Date: 10/7/15

J 690.023 PER
Perish, Patrick,
Skyscraper builder /

SKYSCRAPER BUILDER

BY PATRICK PERISH

BELLWETHER MEDIA · MINNEAPOLIS, MN

Are you ready to take it to the extreme?
Torque books thrust you into the action-packed world
of sports, vehicles, mystery, and adventure. These books
may include dirt, smoke, fire, and dangerous stunts.
WARNING: read at your own risk.

Library of Congress Cataloging-in-Publication Data

Perish, Patrick, author.
  Skyscraper Builder / by Patrick Perish.
     pages cm. -- (Torque. Dangerous Jobs)
  Includes bibliographical references and index.
  Summary: "Engaging images accompany information about skyscraper builders. The combination of high-interest subject matter and light text is intended for students in grades 3 through 7"—Provided by publisher.
  Audience: Ages 7-12.
  ISBN 978-1-62617-197-8 (hardcover : alk. paper)
  1. Skyscrapers--Vocational guidance--Juvenile literature. 2. Construction workers--Juvenile literature. I. Title.
  TH1615.P47 2015
  690'.383023--dc23
                        2014034779

This edition first published in 2015 by Bellwether Media, Inc.

Printed in the United States of America, North Mankato, MN.

TABLE OF CONTENTS

CHAPTER 1

HIGH WINDS

High above the city, a crane lifts a steel beam for a new skyscraper. Skyscraper builders help guide the beam into place. Suddenly, heavy winds begin to blow. One builder loses his footing and slips over the edge.

safety
harness

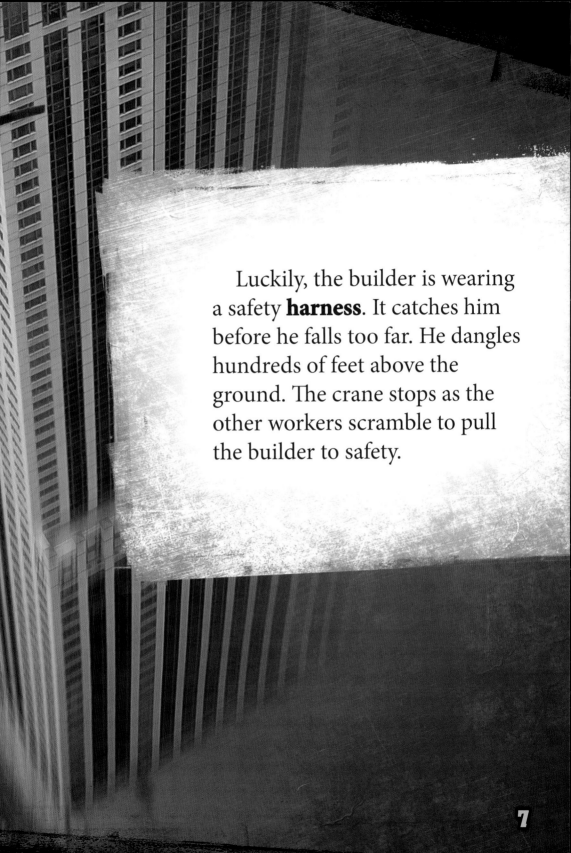

Luckily, the builder is wearing a safety **harness**. It catches him before he falls too far. He dangles hundreds of feet above the ground. The crane stops as the other workers scramble to pull the builder to safety.

CHAPTER 2

SKYSCRAPER BUILDERS

It takes many different workers to build the world's tallest buildings. **Excavator operators** dig up the ground. Next, **foundation** workers place steel poles deep into the earth. They cover these with **concrete** to make a strong base. Then, **ironworkers** use cranes to move iron and steel beams into place.

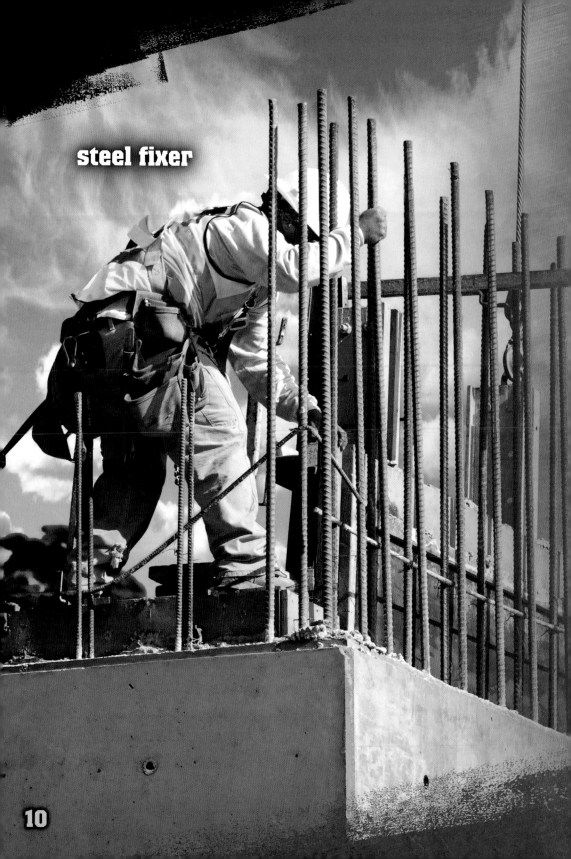

steel fixer

Steel fixers add rods to the building's frame. These are covered in more concrete. As the frame is finished, laborers build the outer walls. Then **finishing crews** add the final touches to the inside of the skyscraper.

One Large Crew

Over 12,000 builders worked every day on a skyscraper called the Burj Khalifa in Dubai. This towering building is 2,717 feet (828 meters) tall and took about six years to finish. It is currently the world's tallest building.

Skyscraper builders are trained on the job by more experienced workers. They are closely guided for three to four years. They learn to read **blueprints** and use tools safely. They also take classes to study math and construction skills. Many are trained to **weld**.

13

Skyscraper builders need good safety gear. Workers wear goggles, hardhats, and harnesses. Safety nets stick out from many buildings. These try to keep people and **debris** from falling to the ground. Good communication is important for safety. Radios keep workers in touch with others they cannot see.

Safety Not Guaranteed

The first skyscraper builders did not wear safety gear. Builders worked hundreds of feet up without harnesses or nets. They wore regular flat caps instead of hardhats.

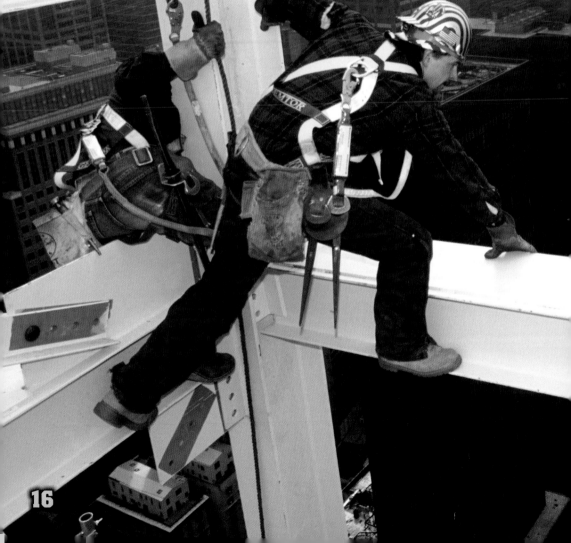

CHAPTER 3

DANGER!

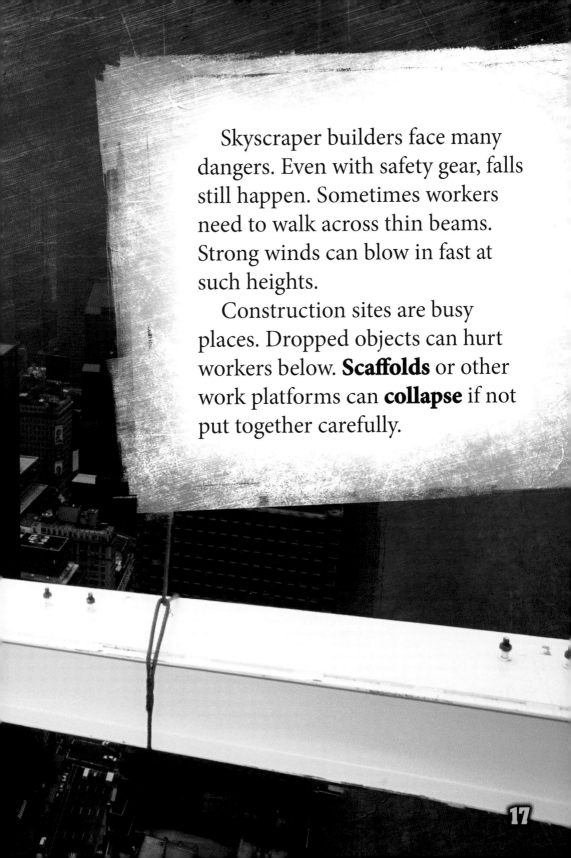

Skyscraper builders face many dangers. Even with safety gear, falls still happen. Sometimes workers need to walk across thin beams. Strong winds can blow in fast at such heights.

Construction sites are busy places. Dropped objects can hurt workers below. **Scaffolds** or other work platforms can **collapse** if not put together carefully.

Skyscraper builders work long shifts. Tired workers can make more mistakes. Sharp and heavy tools may cut or crush workers. Heavy lifting can cause muscle strains.

Builders also face long-term health threats. Breathing in dust from construction sites scars the lungs. Over time, workers can develop **respiratory** problems.

Cover the Eyes

Welders heat steel to around 2,500 degrees Fahrenheit (1,370 degrees Celsius). Welding is so bright it can scar unprotected eyes.

Working on the world's tallest buildings is full of danger. But the jobs pay well and the view is breathtaking. Skyscraper builders love the thrill of being high above the city. Their towering work lasts for decades.

Tragedy on the Job

On January 14, 2008, Yuriy Vanchitskiy and another builder were pouring concrete on the 42nd floor of a New York skyscraper. The platform underneath them suddenly gave way. The other builder landed in the safety netting, but Vanchitskiy fell to his death.

Glossary

blueprints—detailed building plans

collapse—to fall suddenly

concrete—a hard mixture of cement, rock, sand, and water

debris—pieces of garbage or building materials left over from the construction process

excavator operators—workers who use big machines to dig into the ground

finishing crews—groups of workers that add wires, pipes, walls, and other details to complete building a skyscraper

foundation—the base of a building

harness—straps that attach someone to a rope or line

ironworkers—workers who make a building's structure with iron or steel beams

respiratory—relating to the lungs or breathing

scaffolds—platforms used for work on buildings

steel fixers—workers who attach steel bars to the building's structure

weld—to join pieces of metal together using hot torches

To Learn More

AT THE LIBRARY

Didier, Cornille. *Skyscrapers: Who Built That?: An Introduction to Skyscrapers and Their Architects.* New York, N.Y.: Princeton Architectural Press, 2014.

Franchino, Vicky. *How Did They Build That? Skyscraper.* Ann Arbor, Mich.: Cherry Lake Pub., 2010.

Hurley, Michael. *The World's Most Amazing Skyscrapers.* Chicago, Ill.: Raintree, 2012.

ON THE WEB

Learning more about skyscraper builders is as easy as 1, 2, 3.

1. Go to www.factsurfer.com.

2. Enter "skyscraper builders" into the search box.

3. Click the "Surf" button and you will see a list of related web sites.

With factsurfer.com, finding more information is just a click away.

Index